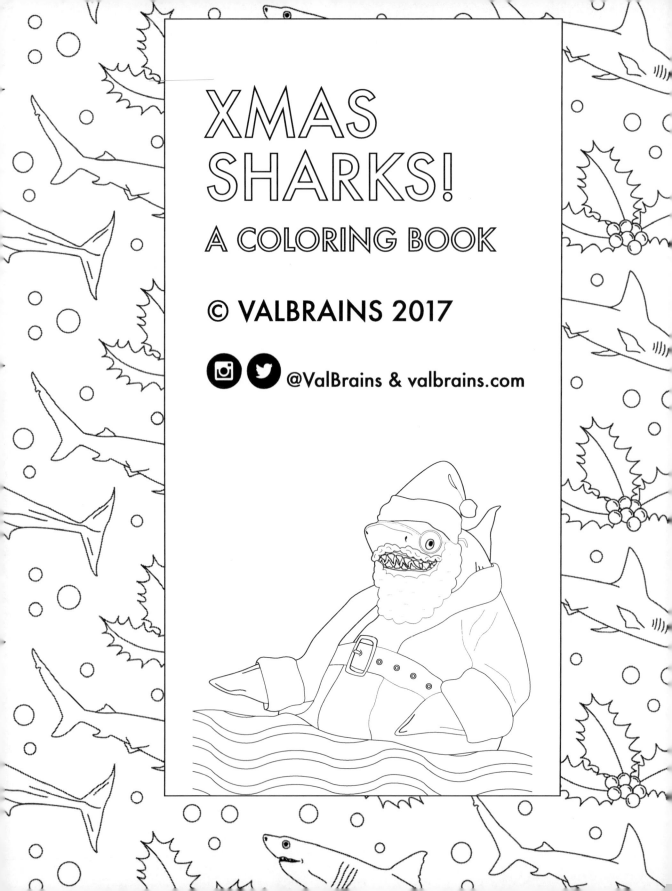

MERRY SHARKMAS!

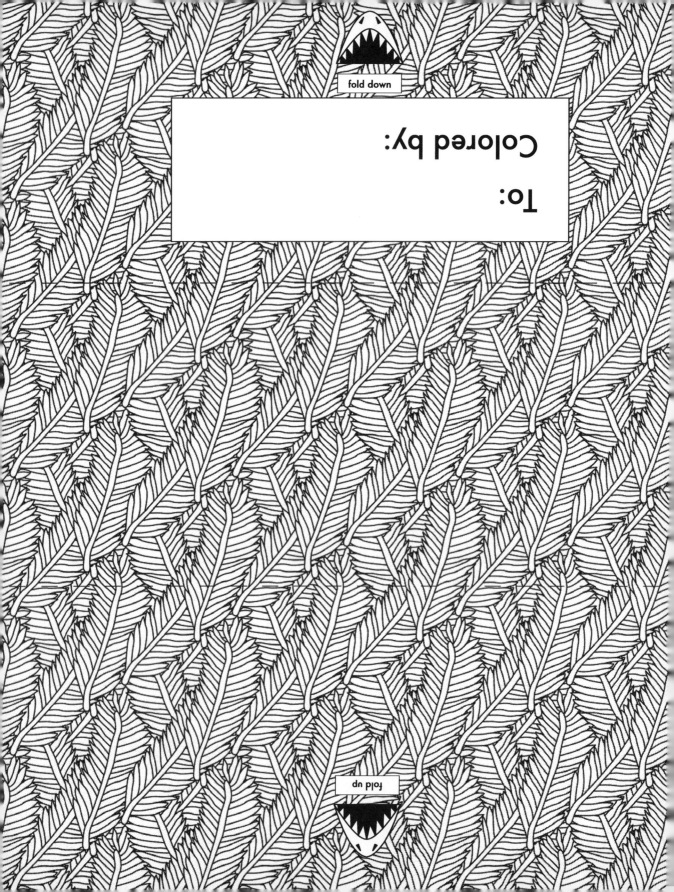

SHARK SMOOCH

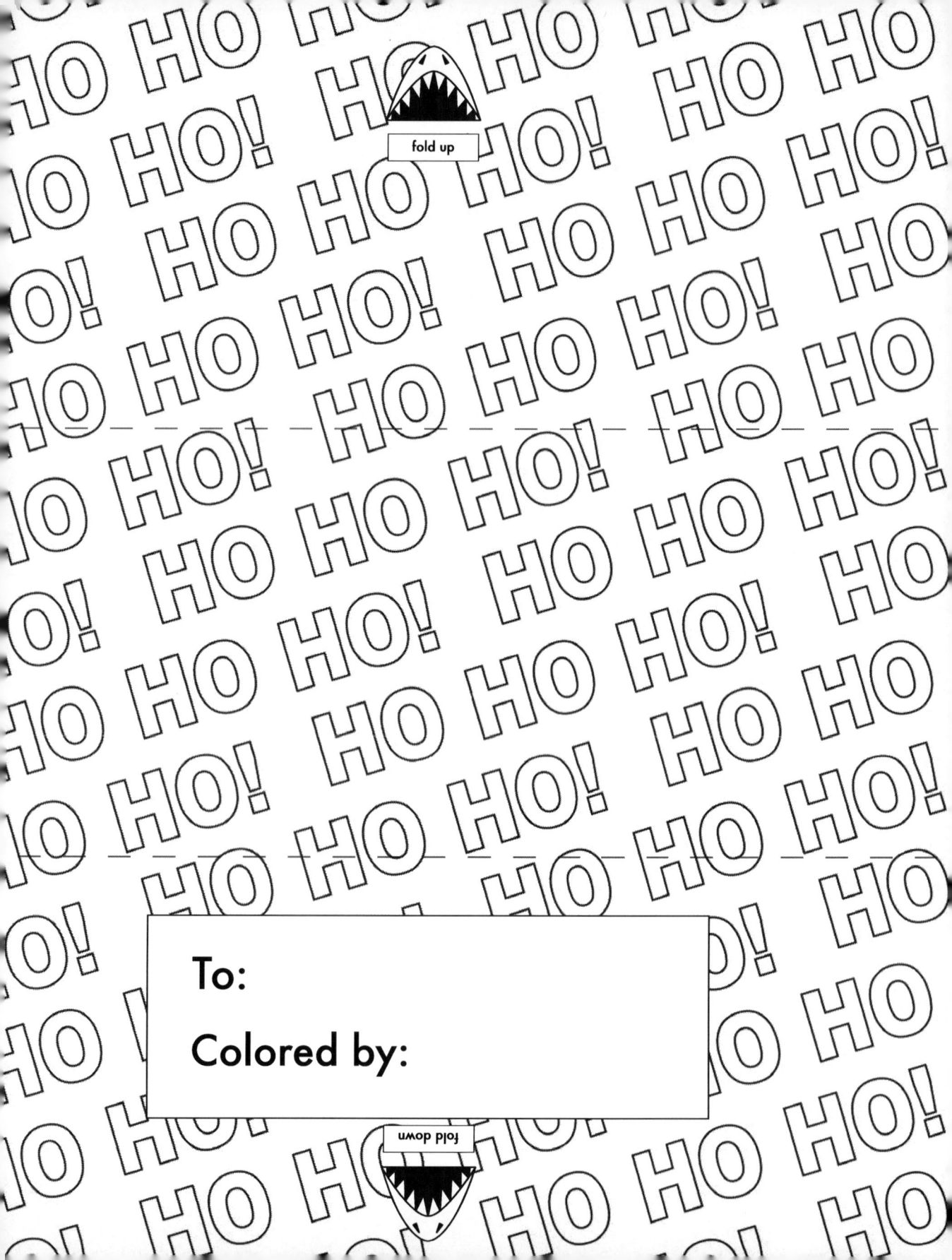

SHARKLE SPARKLE

CANDY CANE CRUNCH

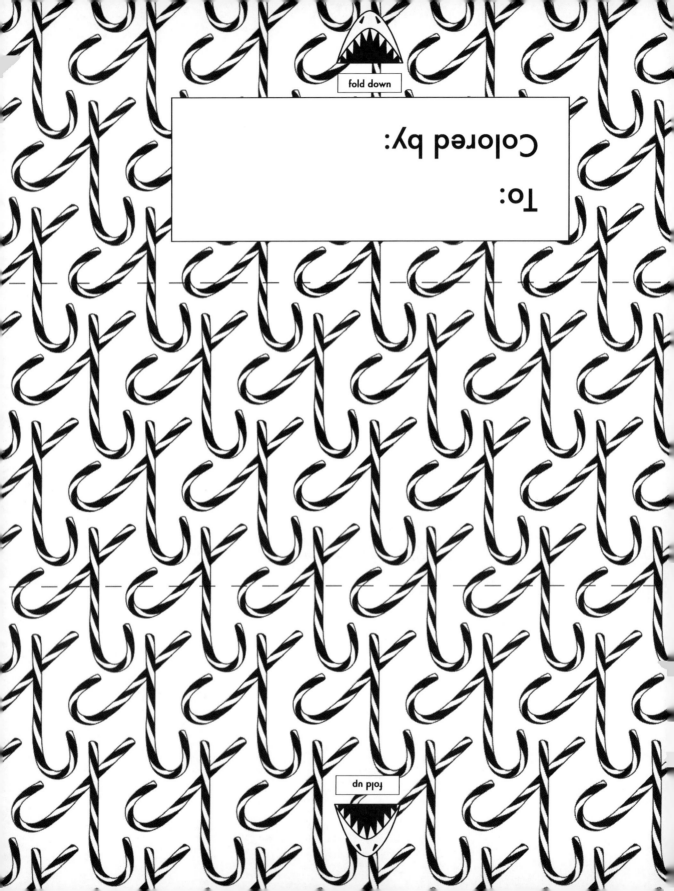

GINGERBREAD SHARK

SHARK NOG

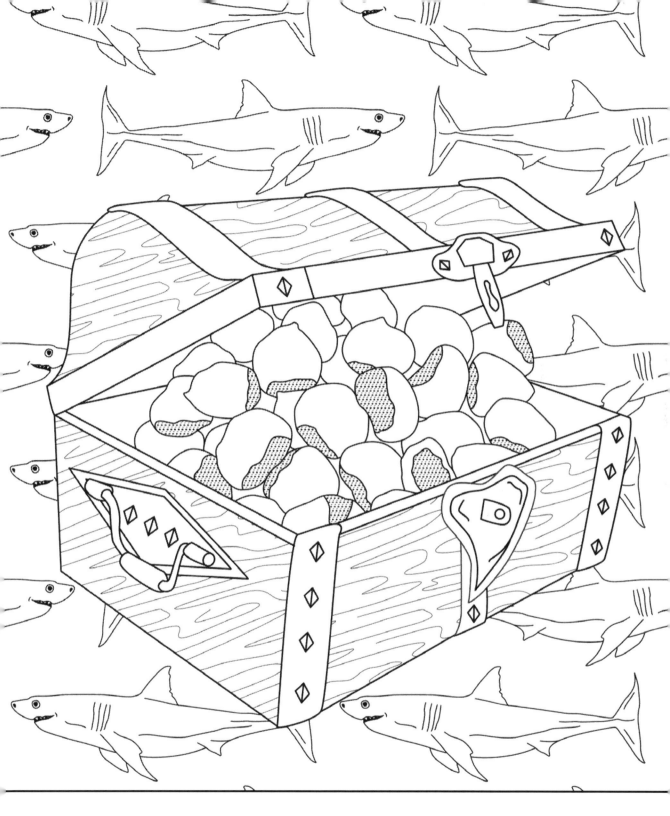

TREASURE CHESTNUTS

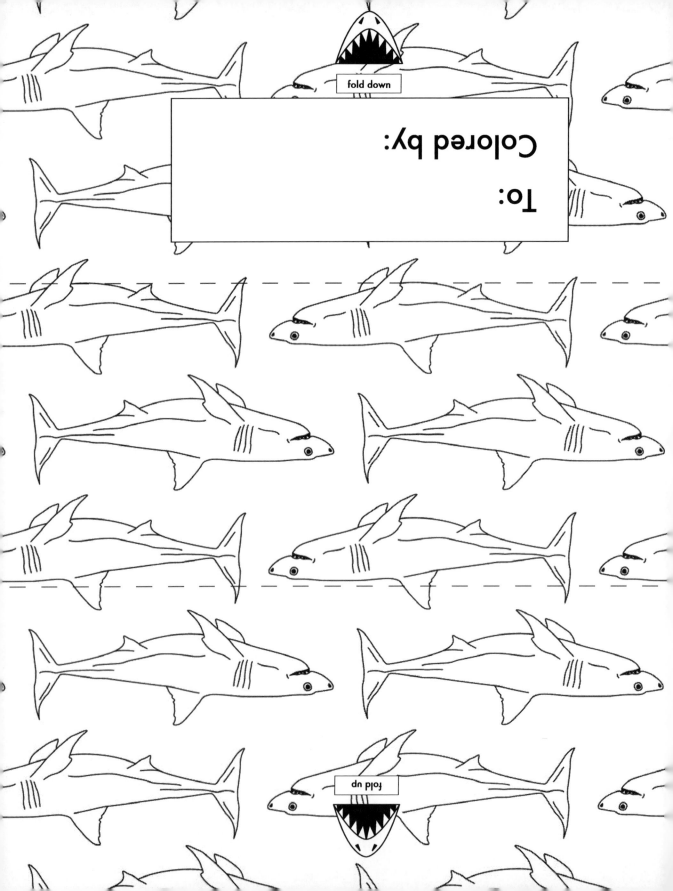

SHARKS OF HOLLY

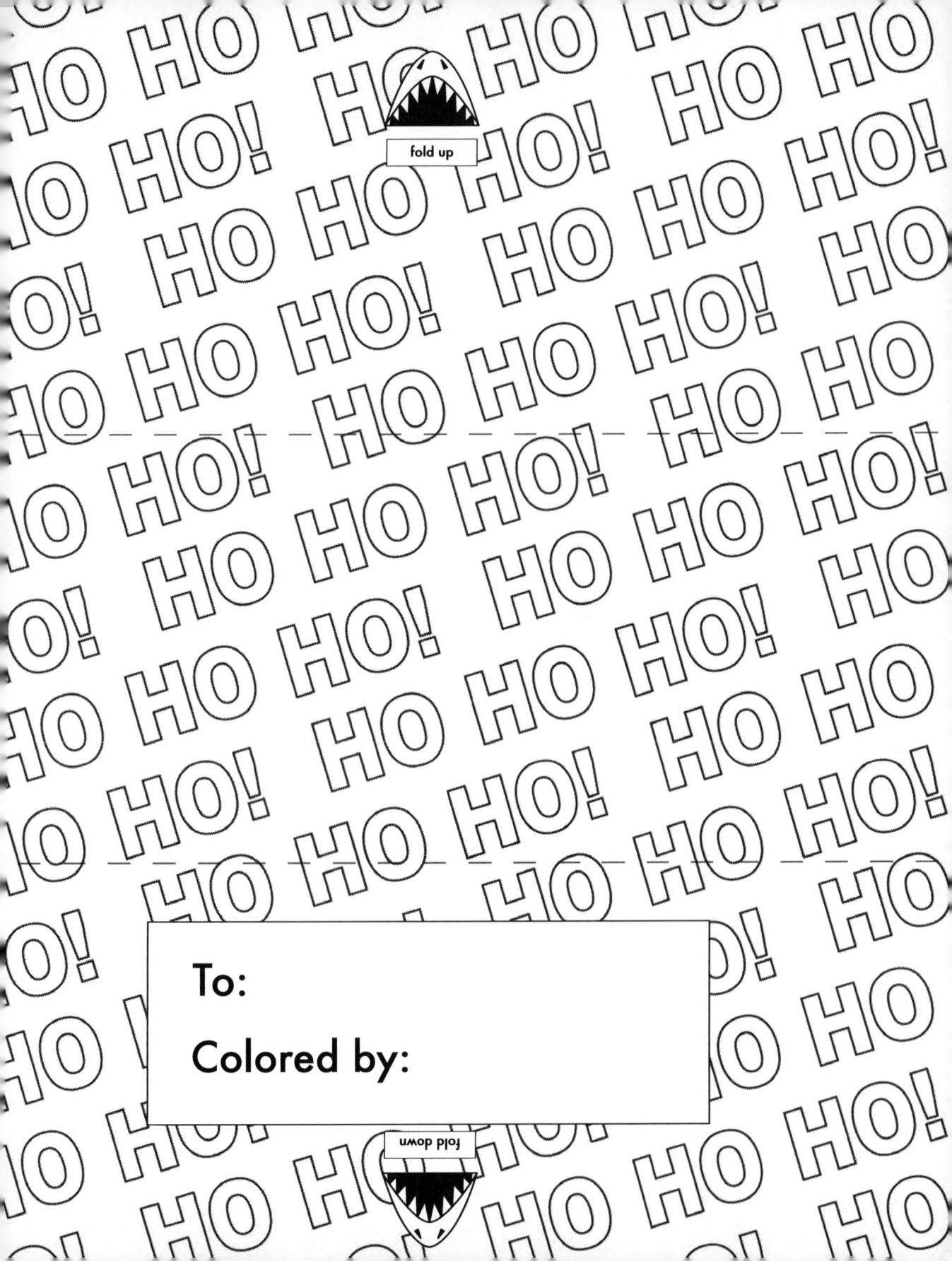

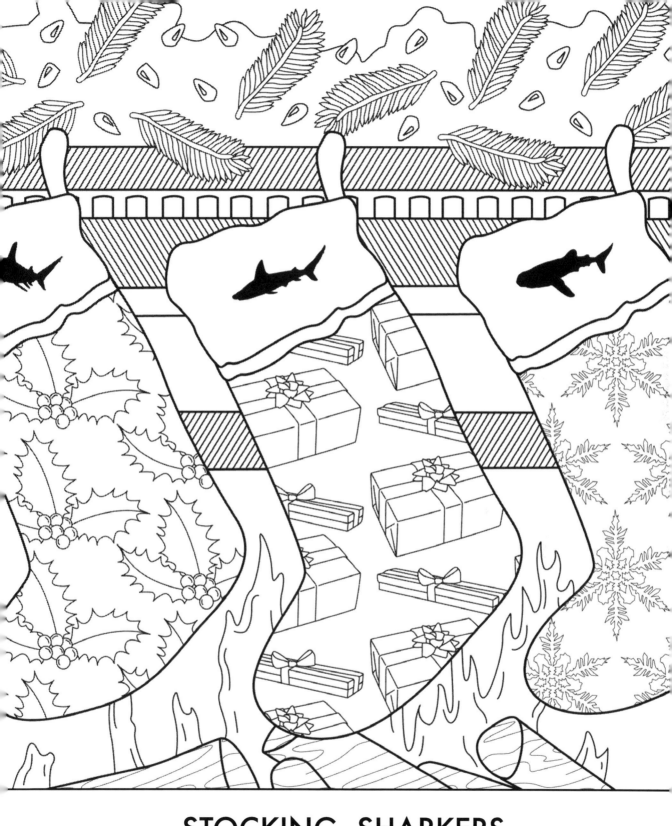

STOCKING SHARKERS

GIFT SHARKS

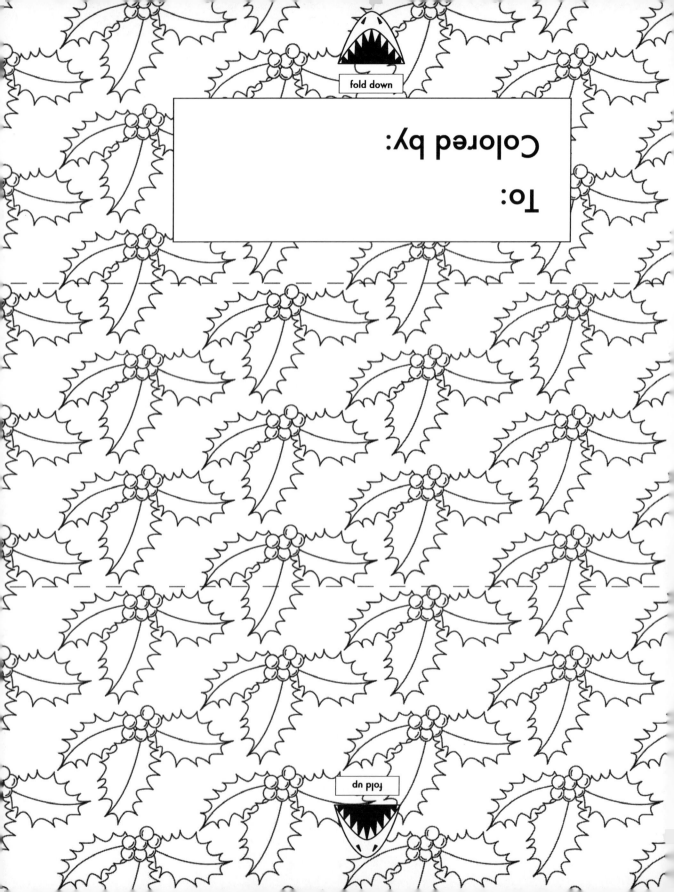

SHARKBOGGAN

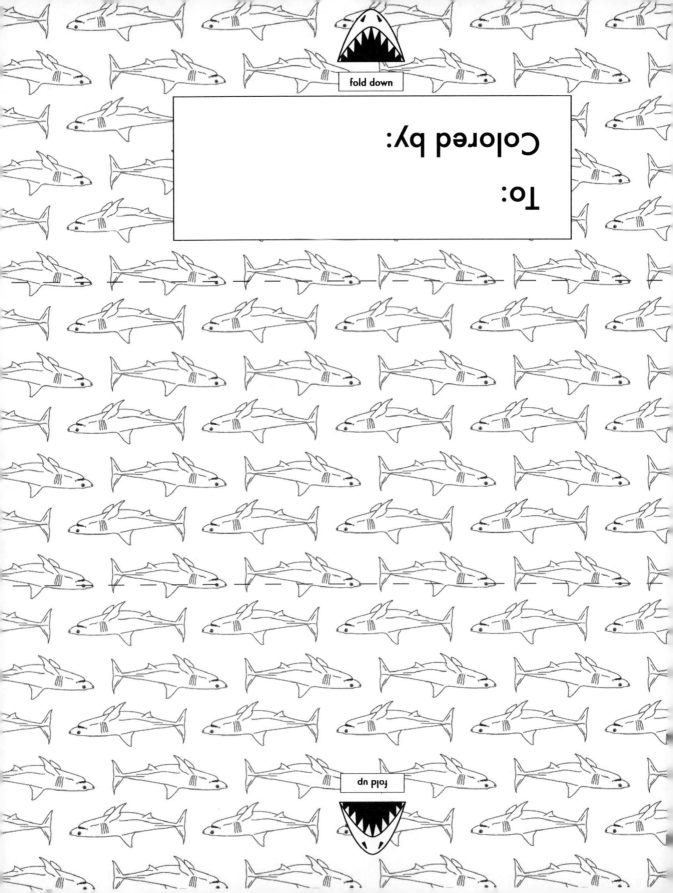

SHARKDOLF

SHARKCITEMENT!

fold up

OMG!

To:

Colored by:

fold down

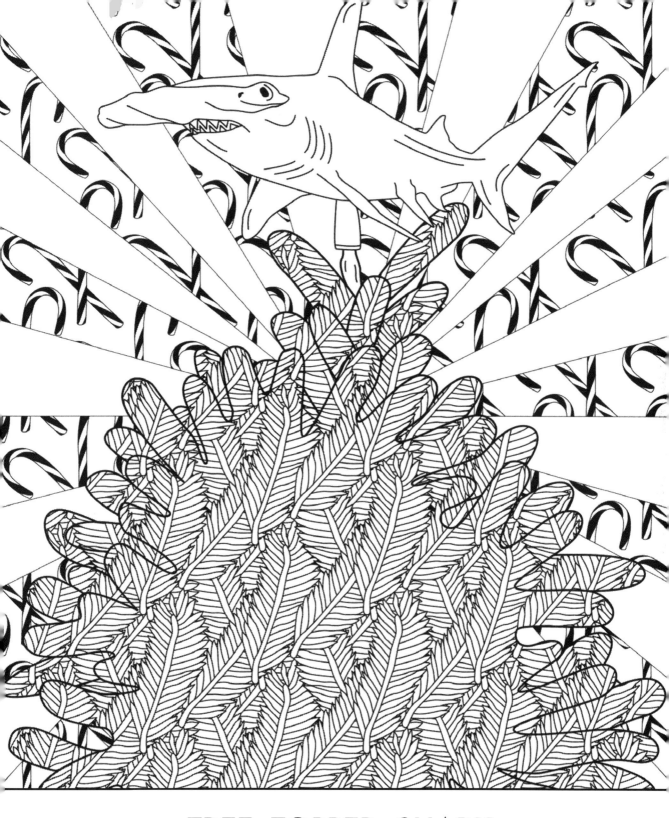

TREE TOPPER SHARK

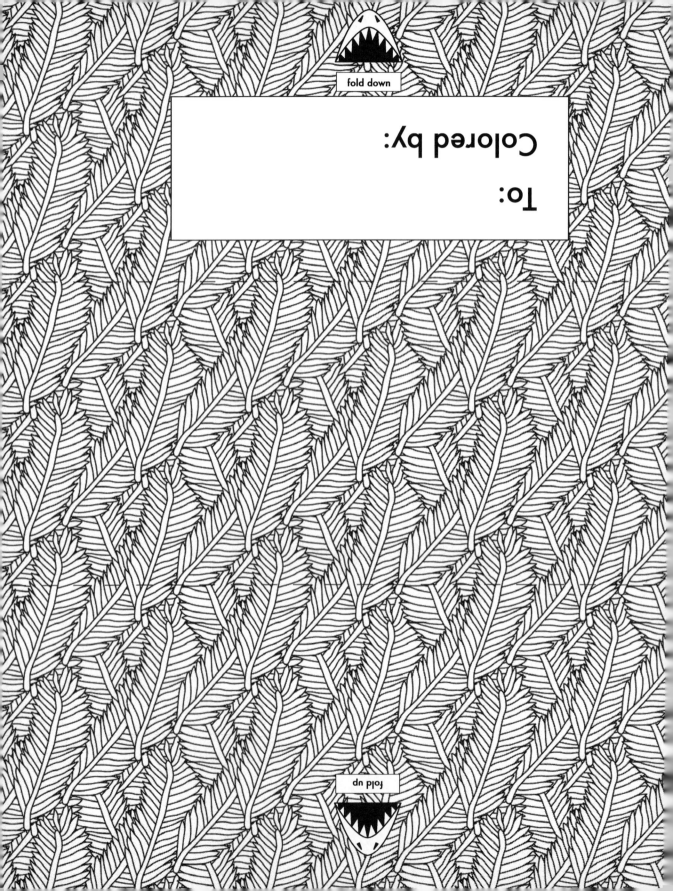

SHARK ON A SHELF

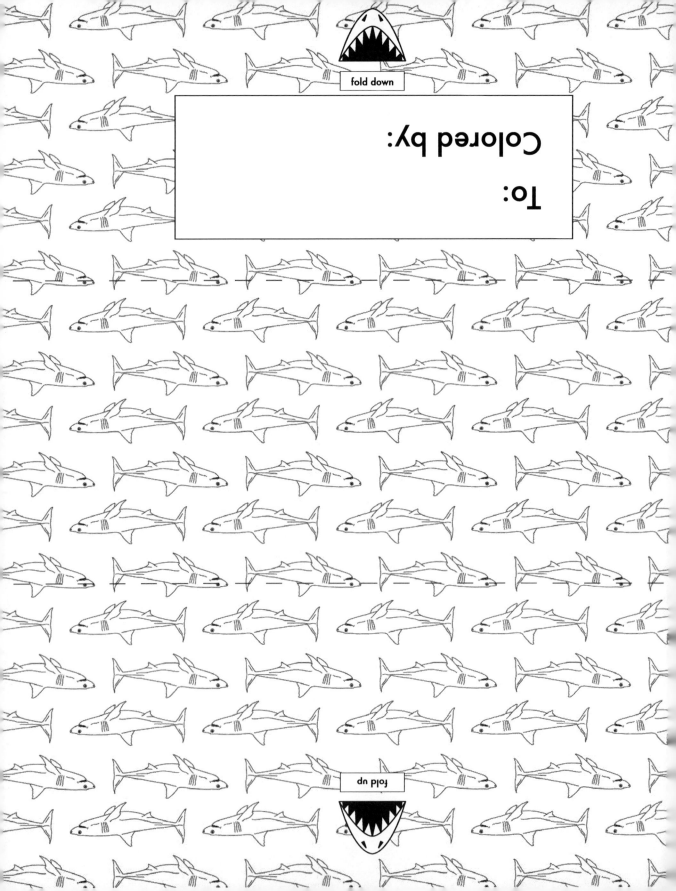

A SHARKMAS STORY

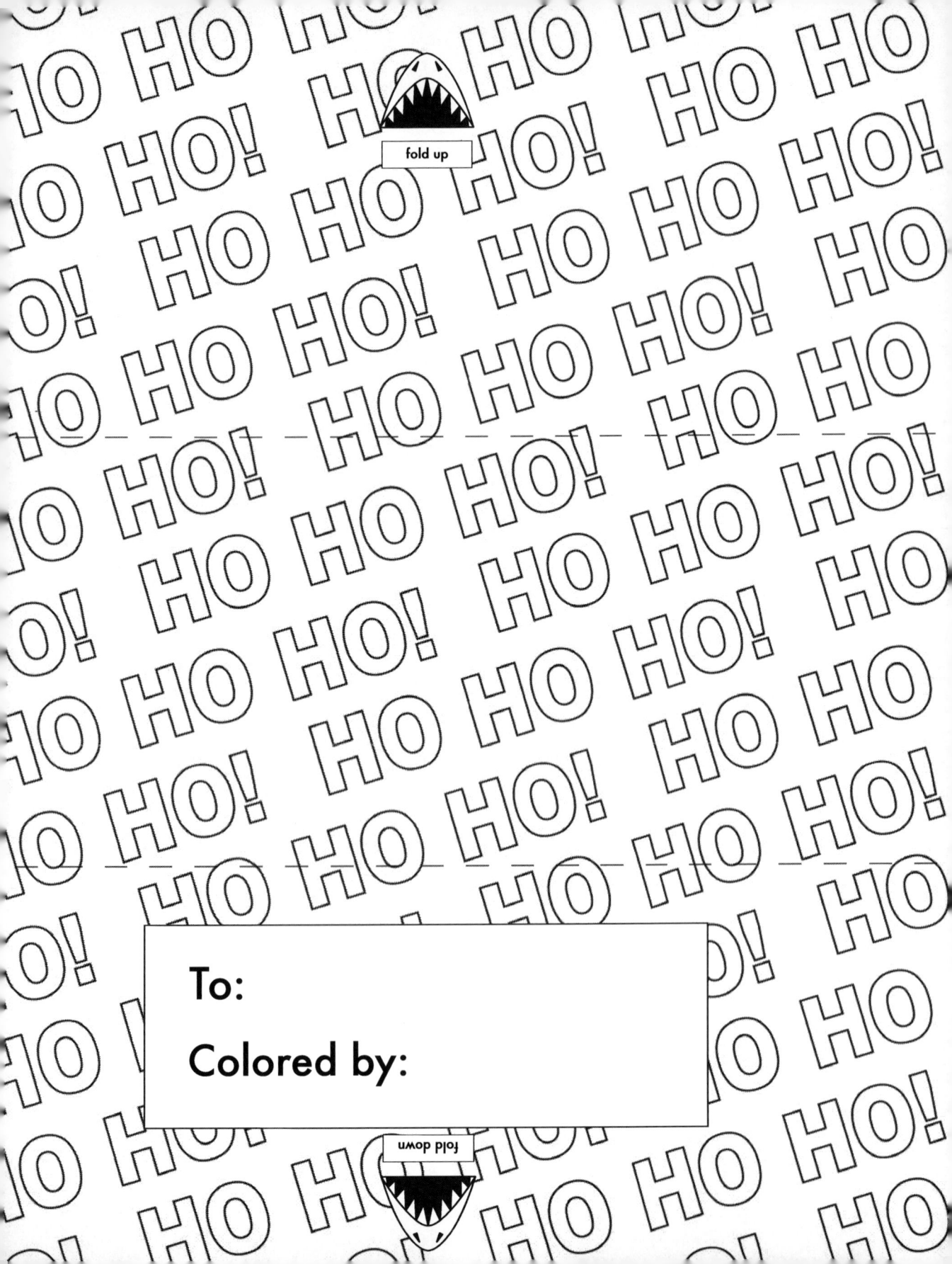

fold up

To:

Colored by:

fold down

UGLY SHARKMAS SWEATER

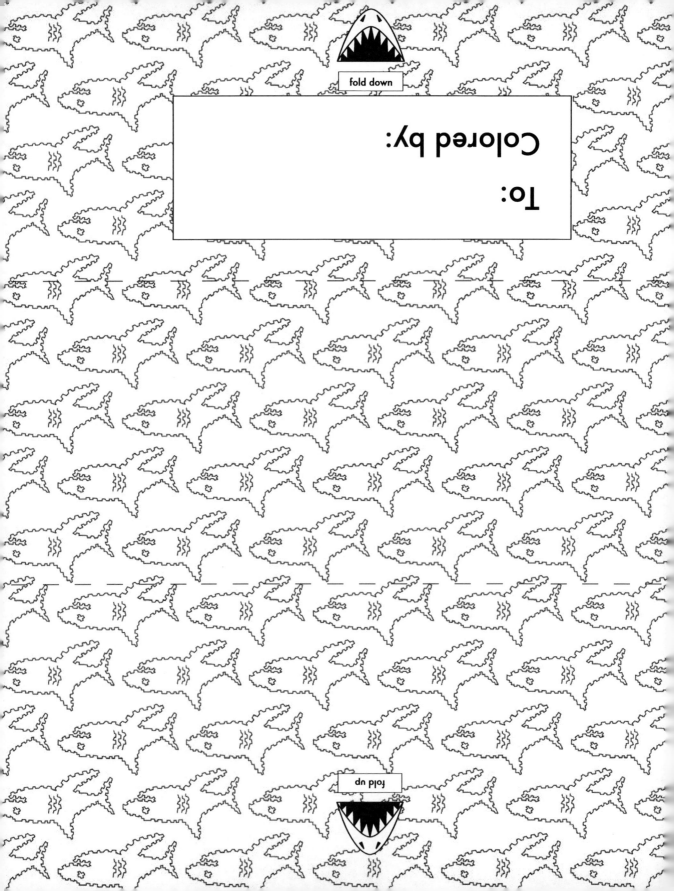

7 SHARKS A-SWIMMING

OBLIGATORY SHARK-DALA

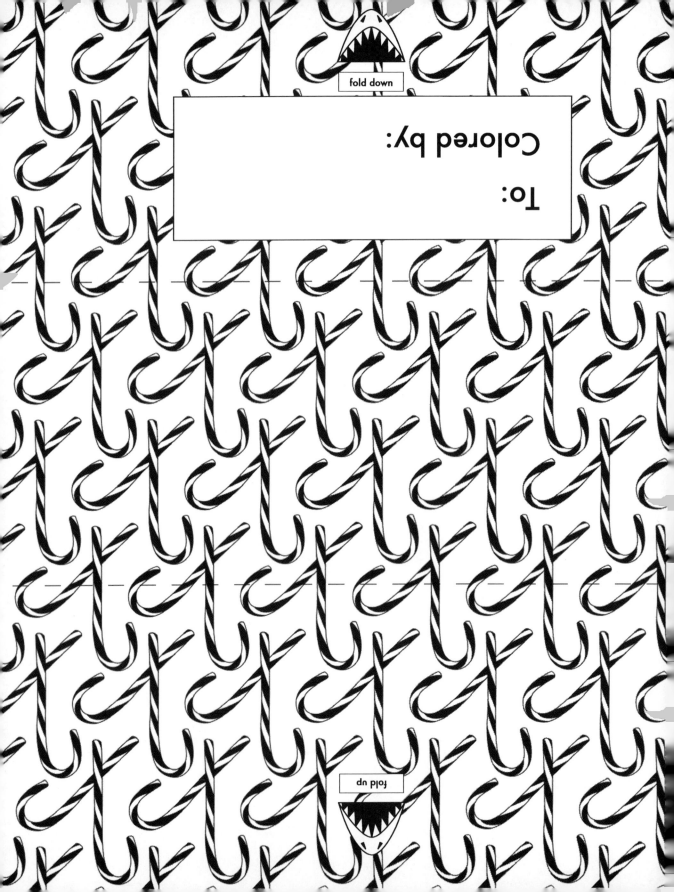

SANTA SHARK!

A XMAS SHARK HAIKU

You may ask yourself:
What beats a regular shark?
A XMAS SHARK, duh!

Printed in Great Britain
by Amazon